A Robbie Reader

What's So Great About...?

FERDINAND MAGELLAN

Jim Whiting

Mitchell Lane
PUBLISHERS

P.O. Box 196
Hockessin, Delaware 19707
Visit us on the web: www.mitchelllane.com
Comments? email us: mitchelllane@mitchelllane.com

Mitchell Lane PUBLISHERS

Printing   1   2   3   4   5   6   7   8   9

A Robbie Reader/What's So Great About . . . ?

Annie Oakley	Daniel Boone	Davy Crockett
Ferdinand Magellan	Francis Scott Key	Henry Hudson
Jacques Cartier	Johnny Appleseed	Robert Fulton
Sam Houston		

Library of Congress Cataloging-in-Publication Data
Whiting, Jim, 1943–
    Ferdinand Magellan / by Jim Whiting.
        p. cm. — (A Robbie Reader. What's so great about . . . ?)
    Includes bibliographical references and index.
    ISBN 1-58415-480-2 (library bound)
    1. Magalhães, Fernão de, d. 1521—Juvenile literature. 2. Explorers—Portugal—Biography—Juvenile literature. 3. Voyages around the world—Juvenile literature. I. Title. II. Series.
    G286.M2W48 2007
    910.92—dc22
    [B]   2006006115

ISBN-10: 1-58415-480-2   ISBN-13: 9781584154808

ABOUT THE AUTHOR: Jim Whiting has been a remarkably versatile and accomplished journalist, writer, editor, and photographer for more than 30 years. A voracious reader since early childhood, Mr. Whiting has written and edited about 200 nonfiction children's books. His subjects range from authors to zoologists and include contemporary pop icons and classical musicians, saints and scientists, emperors and explorers. Representative titles include *The Life and Times of Franz Liszt, The Life and Times of Julius Caesar, Charles Schulz, Charles Darwin and the Origin of the Species, Juan Ponce de Leon, What's So Great About Robert Fulton,* and *The Scopes Monkey Trial.*
        Other career highlights are a lengthy stint publishing *Northwest Runner,* the first piece of original fiction to appear in *Runners World* magazine, hundreds of descriptions and venue photographs for America Online, e-commerce product writing, sports editor for the *Bainbridge Island Review,* light verse in a number of magazines, and acting as the official photographer for the Antarctica Marathon.
        He lives in Washington State with his wife and two teenage sons.

PHOTO CREDITS: Cover—Stefano Blanchetti/Corbis; pp. 1, 3—SuperStock; pp. 4, 11—Library of Congress; pp. 6, 10, 13, 23, 24—Sharon Beck; pp. 7, 26—North Wind Pictures Archives; pp. 8, 18, 20—Getty Images; p. 12—Maritime Museum; p. 22—NASA.

TABLE OF CONTENTS

Words in **bold** type can be found in the glossary.

Ferdinand Magellan is one of the greatest seafarers of all time. His expedition was the first to sail around the world.

Death on the Beach

Ferdinand Magellan was in big trouble. He and about 60 of his men had just come ashore on Mactan, one of the Philippine (FIH-lih-peen) Islands in the Pacific Ocean. The men wore heavy armor and carried sharp lances and swords.

Magellan had left Spain more than a year and a half before. He had sailed thousands of miles and faced many dangers since then. So far, he had succeeded in overcoming all of them.

This time, Magellan had made a serious mistake in judgment. He had offered to help one local chieftain against another one. The rival chieftain was angry.

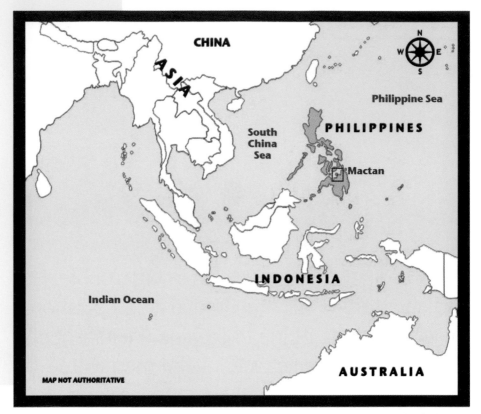

CHINA

ASIA

Philippine Sea

South China Sea

PHILIPPINES

Mactan

INDONESIA

Indian Ocean

MAP NOT AUTHORITATIVE

AUSTRALIA

Magellan landed on Mactan Island in the Philippines. He had pledged to help one local chieftain defeat another. His men were heavily outnumbered by the native army they faced.

He became even angrier when Magellan's men burned some of his people's homes. The chieftain ordered about 1,500 of his men to attack the invaders. Magellan knew he couldn't defeat such a large force. He told his soldiers to retreat. He stood and faced the native army while his men scrambled to safety.

Magellan, dressed in armor, covered the retreat of his men. The native army caught up and killed him.

Magellan didn't have a chance. Standing alone, he was quickly overwhelmed.

Magellan's men were shocked and saddened by his death. He had been a very strong leader. What would happen to them now that he was gone?

In 1493, Pope Alexander VI divided the New World to settle disputes between Spain and Portugal. Each country could control lands in one part. Neither country was satisfied, so the imaginary line the Pope proposed was moved the following year.

Spicing Up the Diet

Ferdinand Magellan was born in Portugal in 1480. In Portuguese, his name is Fernão de Magalhães. After his parents died in 1492, he became a page at the court of Queen Leonor. A page ran errands and did other helpful things for royalty.

In Magellan's time, there was no refrigeration. Food spoiled quickly. To cover up the awful taste, people put pepper and other spices on rotten food. **Europeans** (yur-uh-PEE-uns) imported their spices from Southeast Asia. Arab merchants controlled much of the spice trade. They charged a lot of money for the goods they brought to Europe.

Portugal and Spain are neighboring countries in Europe. They have a long history of territory disputes. In the 1400s and 1500s, both countries were claiming new lands around the world.

The year that Magellan became a page, Christopher Columbus set out to discover a new route to Southeast Asia. If he found one, spices would become cheaper. In 1493, he returned with electrifying news. He had been successful! Columbus's news set off a struggle between the countries of Spain and Portugal.

It would take several years before people realized that Columbus was mistaken. He had

Christopher Columbus plants a flag on the island of San Salvador, claiming the land for Spain. He believed he had sailed all the way to India. He was actually in the Americas.

not found a new route to Asia. He had actually found what would become known as America.

In 1493, Pope Alexander VI divided the world. He used an imaginary line that ran through the Atlantic Ocean. Spain, he declared, would have the right to everything that was discovered west of the line. Portugal would control everything to the east.

Vasco da Gama, a Portuguese explorer, discovered a new way to get to India. He did not sail east as Columbus had. Instead, he sailed south past Africa, then west.

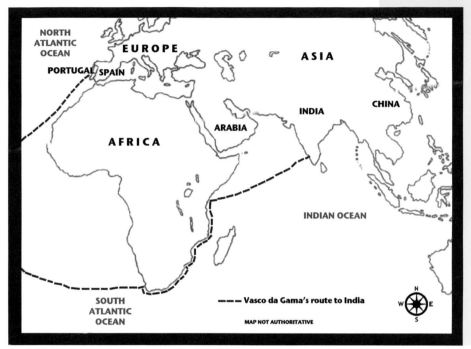

In 1498, Vasco da Gama sailed from Portugal to India. His route rounded the tip of Africa, followed the African coast north, then crossed the Indian Ocean. Magellan followed the same path a few years later.

A few years later, Portuguese captain Vasco da Gama sailed around the southern tip of Africa to India. He had discovered a new way of getting spices. Portugal became wealthy. The country began selling spices to other European countries.

To protect their business, the Arabians fought back. They started attacking Portuguese ships. Magellan wanted to help his country.

Charles I became king of Spain as a teenager. In 1518, he gave Magellan enough money for his expedition to the Spice Islands.

Forming a Bold Plan

In 1505, Magellan joined an **expedition** to Southeast Asia. The group would build forts in Africa and India to help protect Portuguese ships from the Arabians.

Magellan fought in many battles. Once he was seriously wounded. He was promoted to command a ship. He learned about the Spice Islands (today's Molucca Islands), where the spices actually grew. Whoever controlled those islands would gain a big edge in the spice trade. According to his calculations, they were in the part of the world that belonged to Spain.

The Portuguese ruler, King Manuel, was furious. He wanted the Spice Islands for Portugal. He blamed Magellan for the loss. In

1512 or 1513, the king took away Magellan's command and ordered him home. Magellan was disgraced.

Magellan didn't have much money. The king didn't do anything to help him. Instead, Manuel let Magellan go to Morocco to fight. In 1516, Magellan received a severe knee wound. He limped for the rest of his life. When he returned from Morocco, he asked for a small raise in pay. King Manuel refused and **humiliated** him.

Several months later, a friend named John of Lisbon visited Magellan. John had sailed along the coast of South America. He believed there was a passage to India farther down the coast. Magellan grew excited.

Then another old friend came to visit. Duarte Barbosa had served for many years in Asia. Manuel had treated him badly too. Duarte's uncle Diogo was a friend of Spain's new ruler, seventeen-year-old Charles I. The Barbosas thought that Charles would be interested in finding the passage. It was on

Spain's side of the world. They also thought that Magellan would be the perfect leader of an expedition to discover it.

Magellan moved to Spain in 1517. Soon after, he married Diogo Barbosa's daughter Beatriz. They would have one child, a son named Rodrigo.

Barbosa helped set up a meeting between Magellan and Charles. Charles liked Magellan. He also liked Magellan's plan to find the passage. He gave Magellan enough money to buy five ships. They were named *Trinidad, Victoria, Santiago, Concepción,* and *San Antonio.* The ships were less than 90 feet long, yet each one had to hold at least 50 men and all their supplies. It took a year and a half to get ready.

Magellan draws his sword as the native army advances. Some of his men stay to fight, giving the rest the chance to escape.

Through the Passage

Magellan left Spain in September 1519 with about 270 men. He had been very secretive about his **intentions**. No one really knew where he was going. Many of the crew did not trust him. Meanwhile, the fleet had to avoid meeting any Portuguese ships.

After a voyage of three months, Magellan arrived off the coast of South America. As they traveled south, the weather turned very cold. Still they couldn't find the passage. The sailors began to talk of **mutiny** (MYOO-tih-nee). Three of the captains turned against him.

Most of Magellan's men remained loyal to him. He regained control and kept searching for the passage. The *Santiago* sank during the

Magellan guides his ships through the passage. He named it the Strait of All Saints.

search. In October 1520, they finally found it. It was a narrow, winding channel around the southern tip of South America. Magellan named the passage the **Strait** of All Saints.

Once they were in the Pacific Ocean, Magellan thought they had overcome the most important **obstacle**, but another problem arose. The captain of the *San Antonio* had taken the ship back home. She carried most of the food.

The Strait of All Saints was renamed the Strait of Magellan. It snakes between Chile and Tierra del Fuego, which means "Land of Fire." Magellan named Tierra del Fuego when he saw what he believed were the many fires of native peoples in their villages.

At first Magellan wasn't concerned. He believed the Spice Islands were only a few days away. He was wrong. The earth was much bigger than anyone had known.

Magellan sailed for nearly three months without seeing anything. His men ate sawdust, leather, insects, and rats. The drinking water turned yellow. Most of the men got sick, and

A satellite photo of the Strait of Magellan. The snow on the mountains shows how cold the region is. This tip of South America is very close to Antarctica.

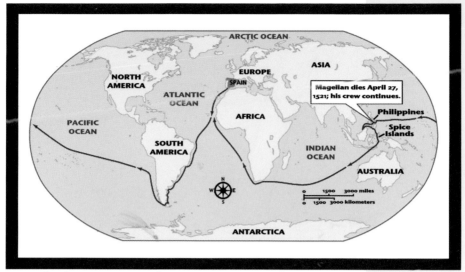

Magellan's route went from Spain to South America, south through the Strait of All Saints, then west through the Pacific Ocean to the Philippines. After Magellan's death in April 1521, another captain took charge. The expedition continued to the Spice Islands and then westward again, back to Spain.

almost twenty died. Finally he found an island with food and water.

He continued sailing west. In mi-March 1521, he arrived in the Philippines. There was plenty of food and water. The men recovered their strength. Soon Magellan was ready to sail to the Spice Islands. They were only a few weeks away.

On the morning of April 27, Magellan was killed in battle on the island of Mactan.

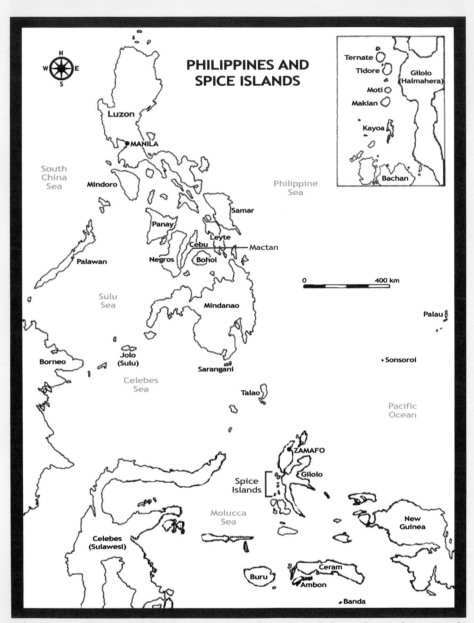

PHILIPPINES AND SPICE ISLANDS

Luzon

●MANILA

South China Sea

Mindoro

Philippine Sea

Samar

Panay

Leyte

Cebu — Mactan

Negros Bohol

Palawan

Sulu Sea

Mindanao

Palau

Jolo (Sulu)

Borneo

Sonsoroi

Sarangani

Celebes Sea

Talao

Pacific Ocean

ZAMAFO

Gilolo

Spice Islands

Molucca Sea

New Guinea

Celebes (Sulawesi)

Buru

Ceram

Ambon

Banda

0   400 km

Ternate

Tidore

Gilolo (Halmahera)

Moti

Makian

Kayoa

Bachan

After Magellan was killed on Mactan, his men did not have far to sail to reach the Spice Islands. It took them six months to find them. For most of the *Trinidad* crew, the Spice Island of Ternate would be their final destination.

The Spice Islands
—and Home

Without Magellan's leadership, it took the expedition six months to find the Spice Islands. More men died or became seriously ill. There weren't enough people to safely operate three ships, so they used just two. The men were divided between *Trinidad* and *Victoria*. *Concepción* was burned.

The two ships took on cargoes of precious spices. The captains decided to split up. *Trinidad* would return the same way they had come. *Victoria* would go west around Africa and head north through the Atlantic.

Trinidad was captured by the Portuguese. The crewmen were thrown into prison on the

The *Victoria* was one of Magellan's five ships. It was the only one to complete the voyage around the world.

Spice Island of Ternate (ter-NAH-tee). Only four of them ever returned to Spain.

   Victoria was more fortunate. She managed to **elude** the Portuguese and finally arrived home in September 1522. Under the command of Juan Sebastián del Cano, *Victoria* was the first ship to sail around the world. Only eighteen men were still alive. One was Antonio Pigafetta, who had kept a detailed **diary** of the

Ternate is one of the Spice Islands. Some of Magellan's men were captured and imprisoned there.

entire voyage. His diary is how historians know so much about what happened.

Magellan did not personally sail around the world, yet he is still given credit for the accomplishment. It was his idea, and he held the expedition together during the most difficult periods. Today he is considered one of the most famous sea explorers of all time. The Strait of All Saints was renamed to honor his memory. It is known as the Strait of Magellan.

CHRONOLOGY

1480   Ferdinand Magellan is born in Portugal.

1492   He becomes a page at the court of Queen Leonor.

1505   Magellan sails to Southeast Asia.

1512 or
  1513   He returns to Portugal in disgrace.

1516   He suffers a severe knee wound in a battle in Morocco.

1517   Magellan leaves Portugal and moves to Spain. He marries Beatriz Barbosa.

1518   He convinces King Charles of Spain to finance an expedition to the Spice Islands.

1519   He sails from Spain to search for a faster route to the Spice Islands.

1521   Magellan is killed at Mactan Island in the Philippines.

1522   The *Victoria,* captained by Juan Sebastián del Cano, completes Magellan's voyage around the world.

TIMELINE IN HISTORY

1488   Bartolomeu Dias sails around the southern tip of Africa.

1492   Christopher Columbus discovers the Americas.

1497   John Cabot searches for a northern passage to India and explores the coast of Canada.

1498   Vasco da Gama establishes a sea route from Portugal to India around the southern tip of Africa.

1502   Columbus begins his fourth voyage to the New World.

1513   Juan Ponce de Leon discovers Florida.

1519   Hernando Cortés lands in Mexico; he conquers Mexico two years later.

1524   Giovanni da Verrazano discovers New York Bay while searching for a northern passage to India.

1539–1542   Hernando de Soto explores Florida and crosses the Mississippi River.

1565   Pedro Menendez de Avilés founds St. Augustine, the oldest city in the United States.

1577–1580   English seafarer Francis Drake sails around the world.

1609   Henry Hudson discovers the Hudson River in modern-day New York.

FIND OUT MORE

Books

Burgan, Michael. *Ferdinand Magellan: The First Trip Around the World*. Minneapolis: Compass Point Books, 2001.

Humble, Richard. *The Voyage of Magellan*. New York: Franklin Watts, 1988.

Kaufman, Mervyn D. *Ferdinand Magellan*. Mankato, Minnesota: Capstone Press, 2004.

Kramer, Sydelle. *Who Was Ferdinand Magellan?* New York: Grosset & Dunlap, 2004.

Works Consulted

Bergreen, Lawrence. *Over the Edge of the World: Magellan's Terrifying Circumnavigation of the Globe*. New York: HarperCollins, 2003.

Humble, Richard. *The Seafarers: The Explorers*. Alexandria, Virginia: Time-Life Books, 1978.

Morison, Samuel Eliot. *The Great Explorers: The European Discovery of America*. New York: Oxford University Press, 1978.

On the Internet

National Maritime Museum: "Ferdinand Magellan: The First to Go Around the World"
http://www.nmm.ac.uk/site/request/
setTemplate:singlecontent/contentTypeA/conWebDoc/
contentId/142

Social Studies for Kids: Ferdinand Magellan
http://www.socialstudiesforkids.com/subjects/magellan.htm

GLOSSARY

diary (DIE-uh-ree)—A personal record of events with entries made at regular intervals.

elude (ee-LOOD)—To avoid capture.

Europeans (yur-uh-PEE-uns)—People who live in Europe, a large area of the earth that includes the countries of England, Spain, Portugal, France, and others.

expedition (ek-spuh-DIH-shun)—A journey taken for a particular purpose; the group of people on such a journey.

humiliate (hyoo-MIH-lee-ayt)—To make someone feel in a lower position.

intentions (in-TEN-shuns)—What one plans to do or to bring about.

mutiny (MYOO-tih-nee)—A revolt against the leader of an expedition or the captain of a ship.

obstacle (OB-stih-kul)—Something that gets in the way.

strait (STRAYT)—A narrow passage that connects two much larger bodies of water.

INDEX